MR. FLEM

MUSHROOM PACIFIC NORTHWEST FORAGING GUIDE

A 5-Step Mushroom Field Guide for Identification, Harvesting, and Preparing Edible Pacific Northwest Mushrooms

DIY MUSHROOM SERIES

Fleming's

STEPHEN FLEMING

Disclaimer

- The objective of the book is simply to provide information; it is not intended to replace diagnosis and treatment, tasks which pertain to a doctor.

- The contents of this book are for informational purposes and are not intended to offer personal medical advice.

- You should seek the advice of your physician or another qualified health provider regarding a medical condition. Never disregard professional medical advice or delay seeking it because of something you have read in this book. The book does not recommend or endorse any products.

- Any book, video, or other means of learning can't replace learning physically from an expert. These forms of information are only additional guidance to be used along with a practical demonstration and training.

- Always check the legal status of the plant you intend to forage and use.

CHAPTERS

Chapter 1: Understanding the Mushrooms - Mycology 101

- *Understanding the Basics of Fungi*
- *Mushroom Anatomy*
- *Benefits Of Mushrooms*

Chapter 2: Five Golden Steps towards Foraging

- *Step 1: Keep An Open Mind*
- *Step 2: Learn To Identify*
- *Step 3: Eliminate All Doubt*
- *Step 4: Right Equipment*
- *Step 5: Harvest*

Chapter 3: Let's Meet Common Wild Mushrooms

- *Edible Mushrooms*
- *Inedible or Poisonous Mushrooms*

Chapter 4: Preserving and Storing Mushrooms

Chapter 5: Let's Cook!

Wild Mushroom Recipes

- *Mushroom Chutney/Salad*
- *Split-gill Mushroom Tea*
- *Wild Mushrooms with Breadcrumbs, Garlic, and Chili*
- *Simple Sautéed Chanterelle Mushrooms*
- *Gorgonzola and Wild Mushroom Risotto*
- *Mushroom Sauce*
- *Creamy Chanterelle Mushroom Soup*
- *Fresh Porcini or Bolete Julienne*

Chapter 6: Seasonal Calendar!

Conclusion

Appendix - Mushroom Identification Logbook Pages

Introduction

Have you ever noticed mushrooms cropping up on the bark of trees and logs in the wild? Did you wonder if they were edible? Do you want to forage mushrooms but are overwhelmed given the wide variety that's available? Well, different types of edible mushrooms can be found in the wild. The key is to identify them before harvesting and consuming.

There are over a million fungi known to us, and many more are yet to be studied and explored. Fungi have an intricate and fascinating life cycle, and they are way more than a nutritious addition to your meals.

They play a crucial role in our environment because they let plants obtain nutrients and moisture from the soil. Apart from it, they break down organic matter and release nutrients to plants. They are also used in different medicines to fight infections, improve the effectiveness of specific treatments, and strengthen the immune system.

The Pacific Northwest refers to the geographic region characterized by various mountain ranges. The geographical areas stretching from Northern California, Oregon, Idaho, and Washington to British Columbia are the Pacific Northwest.

These areas experience mild summers, plenty of rain, and lush green forests. These natural factors create the perfect environment for mushrooms.

Foraging is not a new concept and has been a part of human evolution since the dawn of civilization.

Our prehistoric ancestors survived by foraging and hunting. Foraging refers to identifying, gathering, and harvesting edible flowers, plants, mushrooms, or leaves found in the wild. It is a great way to reconnect with nature, get some exercise, spend more time outdoors, and learn about the local ecosystem.

Foraging becomes even more interesting when you start looking for edible mushrooms. Whether they are oyster mushrooms, morels, or king boletes, different species of edible mushrooms are found in the wild.

Photo by Maria Orlova:
https://www.pexels.com/photo/crop-woman-showing-fresh-mushroom-near-river-in-forest-4906153/

Pacific North West

Foraging mushrooms is a rewarding experience because they make a wonderful addition to any meal. Apart from this, certain mushrooms also have medicinal properties.

Before starting foraging, it is essential to correctly identify the different types of mushrooms, learn to distinguish them from their poisonous lookalikes and inedible mushrooms, and harvest and prepare them properly.

If you are looking for a concise book on mushrooms of the region, *"Mushrooms of the Pacific Northwest Foraging Guide: A 5-Step Mushroom Field Guide for Identification, Harvesting, and Preparing Edible Pacific Northwest Mushrooms "* is the perfect book for you.

This book will act as your guide every step of the way. It will teach you the five basic steps needed to effectively, sustainably, and ethically harvest mushrooms found in the wild. Apart from this, you will also discover delicious recipes you can cook using the foraged mushrooms.

So, are you eager to learn more about all this? If yes, there is no time like the present to get started!

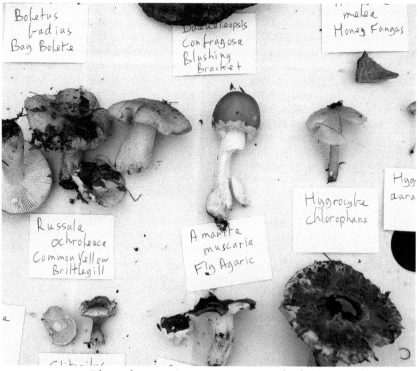

Photo by Annie Spratt on Unsplash

1. Understanding the Mushrooms – Mycology 101

You might have eaten or cooked with mushrooms. Chances are, you might have also seen some in the wild. Perhaps you think of oyster mushrooms, chanterelles, or morels when you hear the word mushrooms. However, there are so many more varieties than just these. The use of mushrooms is not just restricted to culinary purposes.

They are incredibly diverse, beneficial, and have a variety of attractive characteristics. A mushroom is the visible fruiting body sprouting from an extensive interconnected network of underground root-like structures. Mushrooms are available in a variety of shapes, sizes, and colors. Some are edible while others are medicinal, and some are edible and, at times, poisonous.

Understanding the Basics of Fungi

Mycology is the study of fungi. It's about understanding their biochemistry and how they relate to other organisms. Recent progress in scientific technology, especially DNA testing, has revealed that fungi are closely related to animals and not plants, as was previously believed. Fungi don't have any chlorophyll; the pigment plants use for producing energy. Most fungi obtain sustenance by metabolizing dead or decaying matter and are classified as saprophytes.

Mushroom is the reproductive structure produced by a specific type of fungi. Mycologists believe there are millions of species of mushrooms yet to be identified.

Did you know that the largest known living organism in the world is Armillaria Ostoyae, and it is a type of fungus?

It covers approximately 4sq.miles and is bigger than the blue whale, the largest known mammal. Only a tiny portion of this humongous fungus is visible. It is estimated that most of its weight is in the form of an underground mycelial network amounting to 35,000 tons!

Mushroom Anatomy

Before you learn to forage mushrooms, understanding their basic anatomy is needed because it helps with better identification. Here are all the different parts of a mushroom.

MUSHROOM ANATOMY

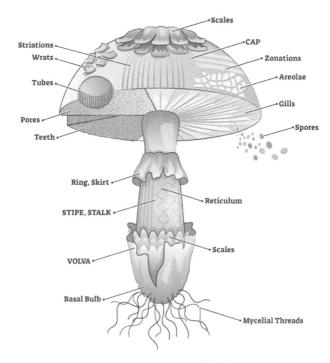

Cap

The top part of the mushroom is known as the cap or the pileus. Whenever you look at the mushroom, this is the first thing that will catch your eye. It is an umbrella or a dome-like structure that protects the spores and gills from the elements.

Gills

Mushrooms have gills that look pretty similar to those of fish. Gills refer to fine teeth-like structures that can be found right under the cap of the mushroom and house their spores.

Spores

Pores are also known as spores and are a means of propagation for mushrooms. Spores are present in the gills.

Mycelium

The roots of plants usually dig deep into the ground to find the nutrition they require. Even mushrooms have fine hair-like strands that dig into the soil to obtain the nutrients they need. These structures are known as mycelium. The function of mycelium in mushrooms is the same as roots in plants. The fine filament-like structures the mycelium is made of are known as hyphae.

Fruiting Body

The entire mushroom that grows from the mycelium is referred to as its fruiting body, and it contains the cap, gills, volva, stipe, and veil.

Stipe

This is also known as the stem of the mushrooms, and it's the vertical portion upon which the cap sits. It is also visible above the surface.

Ring

The ring is the annulus of the mushroom and is a small part of the veil left behind on its stem. As the cap matures, it breaks through the veil, and the leftover pieces in this process form a ring-like structure around the stipe.

Veil

It is an additional layer of protection that ensures the spores are safe while the mushroom is maturing.

Volva

The cap-like structure most mushrooms have close to the base is known as the volva. This is also the leftover bit of the veil that homes the spores.

Benefits Of Mushrooms

Mushrooms offer a variety of benefits. Foraging mushrooms is a great way to obtain these superfoods from nature.

Foraging by itself is a wonderful activity. It can be a hobby, stressbuster, an opportunity to bond with nature, and a reason to learn more about the local ecosystem.

Mushrooms are rich in various antioxidants needed for tackling inflammation and oxidative stress. These are the common causes of cognitive decline and different harmful health conditions.

So, consuming mushrooms is a great way to reduce the odds of cognitive decline. Calcium and vitamin D are two essential nutrients commonly found in mushrooms. These nutrients are needed to maintain and strengthen the skeletal structure's integrity.

In addition, they are filled with B-complex vitamins that are a source of energy. They also contain selenium, calcium, potassium, phosphorus, zinc, choline, potassium, and iron.

Apart from all this, foraging also teaches you more about the local ecosystem and its problems. Understanding all this will automatically make you more environmentally conscious.

Foraging Mushroom with kids

2. Five Golden Steps towards Foraging

Foraging Mushroom in Oregon

Now that you understand and are familiar with the basic biology of mushrooms, it is time to learn foraging. Foraging is not just about heading out into the woods and picking random mushrooms.

It is about understanding the mushrooms you are picking, ensuring they are edible, and harvesting them carefully. Here are the five steps you should follow to start foraging mushrooms.

Step 1: Keep An Open Mind

The first step in learning about foraging mushrooms is to keep an open mind. It means you should never assume that you know everything about mushrooms.

Foraging is not just about picking mushrooms. It's an exciting, beneficial, and engaging activity. Take a moment and think about it. You'll be spending hours walking or hiking in the wild, breathing in the fresh air, and connecting with nature. Apart from this, you might never know; you will probably come across some delicious woodland delicacies that can be later shared with your loved ones.

Foraging is not just about harvesting. You must be conscious and ethical too. It means you should not only know what you are doing but also avoid harming the local landscape. To do this, you must spend some time carefully identifying the likely species you will encounter.

The good news is you no longer have to spend hours searching for the right information. This book will act as your guide and help kickstart the process of learning to become a forager. You should also look at different images and make a mental note of the mushrooms that you can and cannot eat. Apart from that, don't hesitate to share your knowledge with others. The more you learn, the better forager you can become.

Step 2: Learn To Identify

Apart from keeping an open mind to foraging, you should learn to identify different species of mushrooms. Several varieties are fit for consumption. Some are edible, while others are considered gourmet delicacies. That said, several mushrooms are poisonous, toxic, and inedible. Medicinal mushrooms are also different from their edible counterparts. Some can be cooked, while others can be turned into tinctures or powders for medicinal applications.

If you are residing in the Pacific Northwest — the regions of Northern California, Idaho, Washington, Ontario, and British Columbia, different species of mushrooms are found in the wild.

Pacific Northwest Foraging

Some edible mushrooms also have poisonous look-alikes. Unless you learn to identify correctly, foraging will not be a worthwhile experience. After all, what is the point of spending hours searching for mushrooms and harvesting only to realize they are inedible?

In this book, you will be introduced to some common wild edible mushrooms and poisonous varieties you should stay away from.

Step 3: Eliminate All Doubt

One of the essential rules of mushroom foraging is to identify the mushroom and eliminate all doubt. A popular saying among foragers is,

"There are bold mushroom hunters and old mushroom hunters, but there are no old and bold mushroom hunters."

It might sound funny, but it is true. Getting poisoned because you have incorrectly identified a mushroom is a mistake that can prove deadly. Most novice foragers do this, and ensure that you are not one of them.

Certain mushrooms are inedible but not poisonous. It means that you will not die if you eat them unknowingly. Some species can cause flu-like symptoms and trigger nausea, while others can cause severe damage resulting in organ failure.

For instance, the death cap mushrooms can trigger severe liver dysfunction within minutes of consumption. So, learning to differentiate between edible, inedible, and poisonous mushrooms is crucial.

Amanita phalloides or Death Cap Mushroom

It's important to understand that all inedible mushrooms are not poisonous. Certain mushrooms are inedible because of their taste. Whenever foraging, ensure that whatever mushroom you pick is 100% safe for consumption. Even if you have a little doubt, it's better not to eat.

Here are some simple suggestions you should remember to ensure you have correctly identified the mushroom.

Even if you have a little doubt, do not eat the mushroom. Erring on the side of caution is good for your health and wellbeing. So, spend a bit longer to identify the mushroom correctly. You can do this by taking the time to reexamine every mushroom you pick before preparing it separately. You might have unwittingly picked up the wrong species and placed it in the basket at times. Even if it is not poisonous, inedible mushrooms can ruin the flavor of any dish you are trying to cook.

Ensure that the mushrooms picked are from clean spots if you are foraging in urban areas. Mushrooms don't just metabolize dead and decaying matter; they also absorb fertilizers and other harmful chemicals in the ground. If you are not careful, these toxic compounds will enter your body. So, avoid foraging mushrooms next to old dumpsites or busy roads.

Mushroom near polluted site

You don't have to be scared of identifying poisonous mushrooms. The more familiar you are with the species, the more correctly you can identify them. This applies to all mushrooms, including the inedible and poisonous ones. Ideally, wear gloves whenever you're harvesting mushrooms. Certain mushrooms release toxins that cause skin irritation.

Don't be afraid to touch, pinch, feel and smell mushrooms, even if they are poisonous varieties. It is fine as long as you don't eat them and wear gloves while handling them.

Don't be too focused on identifying mushrooms that you forget about your surroundings. It is pretty easy to get lost in the wilderness. Ensure that you take time to get your bearings, so you don't get lost. You must also be aware of other dangerous or toxic plants you might encounter on your foraging expeditions.

Common poisonous species native to the Pacific Northwest include wild carrots, poison oak, deadly hemlock, and stinging nettle.

Poison Oak in wild Oregon
Photo by James Whitney on Unsplash

Deadly Hemlock

Stinging Nettle

Step 4: Right Equipment

Don't roam around in the wild without the proper equipment for harvesting mushrooms. It would help if you also had specific tools for identifying them. For a safe and productive foraging experience, ensure that you have the essential tools discussed here.

Basket

Mushrooms are fragile, and dumping them in a backpack or placing them in a plastic bag is not good. When mushrooms are kept inside plastic bags or containers without air circulation, they become moist and develop a slimy texture. You will need a basket made of natural materials such as wicker and maple veneer or a cloth bag made of breathable porous material.

Knife

You will need a high-quality, sharp knife or blade to harvest mushrooms. After all, ethical foraging is to get what you want from nature without harming or disturbing it too much. Since a bit of digging is involved in harvesting mushrooms, a knife is needed. In addition, mushrooms have to be dug out and examined for proper identification.

Basket & Knife

Brush

The simplest way to gently get rid of any dirt on mushrooms is by using a brush. Using a soft-bristled brush also comes in handy while inspecting the mushrooms.

Magnifying Glass

This comes in handy for examining the spore prints and other finer details used for identifying and distinguishing mushrooms.

Field Guide

Always carry a mushroom field guide with you. Regardless of how certain you are about a mushroom, it's never a bad idea to check again. A field guide with pictures of the common mushrooms found in the Pacific Northwest will help with better identification.

Brush, Magnifying Glass & Field Guide

Permit

A permit is needed if you are foraging on any government property. Usually, if you are foraging for noncommercial purposes and collect only a specific amount of mushrooms daily, the permit is free. A special permit is needed for highly coveted mushrooms such as the matsutake. Get in touch with the local forest department or forest service's ranger station to obtain the required permits. Ensure that you are also informed about the common areas approved for foraging.

Water And Snacks

Foraging mushrooms is an exciting activity. That said, it could also take hours together at times. This is one of the reasons why you should always carry plenty of water and snacks before heading into the forest. Apart from dressing for the occasion, ensure that you have sufficient snacks and water to keep you hydrated and satiated. One rule that you should not forget is to not litter in the forest!

GPS Device or Map

It is quite easy to get lost in a dense forest. So, ensure that you always carry an offline GPS device or a map before heading into the wild outdoors.

3. Let's Meet Common Wild Mushrooms

The Pacific Northwest includes the regions of Idaho, Washington, Ontario, and Northern California in the United States and British Columbia in Canada. So, if you live in any of these regions, you have a variety of mushrooms to forage.

However, learning how to identify them is the first step to becoming a good forager. In this chapter, you will not only learn about the common mushrooms found in the wild in the Pacific Northwest, their natural habitat and growing season, and how to identify them. Once armed with this information, foraging for mushrooms will become easy.

Edible Mushrooms

In this section, let's look at the most common types of edible mushrooms found in the Pacific Northwest.

(1) Shrimp Russula

Shrimp Russula or russula xerampelina is an extremely delicious edible mushroom found during the fall in coniferous forests of the Pacific Northwest. This mushroom has a beautiful deep color that can be found in shades of deep purple, brown, olive, red, and pink. The stem is usually white with a slight tint of pink, and it can even have yellow-brown spots on it. The gills are attached to the stem when young and separate as the mushroom matures. The key factor for identifying this mushroom is its smell. It has a shrimp or fish-like odor and hence its name. Depending on the maturity of the mushroom, the order also increases.

It has a convex cap that is smooth and sticky to touch. Their cap can be 6-20cm wide with a 4-12 centimeters long stem. These mushrooms are incredibly brittle and should be handled with care.

Shrimp Russula

Image by PublicDomainPictures from Pixabay

(2) Dark Honey Mushroom

Dark honey mushrooms or armillaria ostoyae are edible mushrooms found during summer and early winters along the Pacific Northwest. They are usually found in coniferous forests.

The cap of these mushrooms is 5-15 centimeters wide with a reddish-brown hue that changes color as it dehydrates and turns pale. When young, the cap is covered with brown scales that smoothen out as it matures.

The cap has white flesh and is firm to touch. The stipe is 6-15 centimeters tall with a wooly texture.

These mushrooms have a double ring on their stipe that is white-colored with black or brown scales. Even though they are known as honey mushrooms, they have an acidic flavor and should be cooked thoroughly before consumption.

Honey Mushrooms

(3) Summer Oyster Mushroom

In coniferous and deciduous forests, summer oyster mushrooms or Pleurotus pulmonarius are found across the Pacific Northwest during late summers and spring.

These delicious mushrooms sport a white or light-tan cap with an incredibly short stipe. In some cases, the stipe might be fully absent too. These mushrooms grow in fan-like clusters and are partial to hardwoods.

Their convex cap can be 5-25 centimeters wide with a fan-like or semi-spherical shape.

The immature cap can be slightly greasy to touch. As it matures, fine lines start appearing on it, and the cap becomes wavier. The gills of this mushroom grow down the stem and are white-colored.

Summer Oyster/Pleurotus pulmonarius

(4) Angel Wings

Angel wings or pleurocybella porrigens is a commonly found wild mushroom in the Pacific Northwest. They are predominantly edible mushrooms but should be avoided by anyone with known kidney disorders. These mushrooms grow in overlapping clusters in conifer forests during fall and late summer. These edible mushrooms are bland per se but can be added to stews and soups.

The cap of this mushroom can be 1.5-10 centimeters wide and can be white ivory or cream-colored. It has a fan-like appearance with crowded gills and an extremely short stipe. The cap of these mushrooms can be shallow petal-shaped and convex. They have white and smooth spore prints. The spore shape is the primary differentiating factor between angel wings and other types of oyster mushrooms.

Oyster mushrooms have cylindrical spores while angel wings have globose spores.

Angel wings / pleurocybella porrigens

(5) Blewit

Blewit or lepista nuda is a highly delicious mushroom sought after in European countries. They commonly grow in coniferous forests and woodlands in winter and fall. The cap can be brown or lilac hued, making them seem almost blueish when young. The stem can be 6-15 centimeters wide, and as it matures, it takes on a tan hue.

The inwardly rolled margins of the cap house crowded gills that are pink or lilac-colored. Its light-purple-colored stem can be 5-10 centimeters long. These mushrooms are pretty simple to identify, especially when young, because of their bluish-purple tinge. Mature varieties of these mushrooms are sometimes found after the first frost in winter too. The spores are ellipsoidal with a pinkish tinge.

Blewit or lepista nuda

(6) Fried Chicken Mushroom

Fried chicken mushrooms or lyophyllum decastes are edible mushrooms commonly found in grassy areas. They grow in dense clusters, especially in areas where the ground has been moved, such as roadbeds and paths.

You can also find them in wooded regions. Their growth is quite prolific through summer and fall. These mushrooms have a cap that is 4-12 centimeters wide and can be beige, brown, off-white, or light brown with golden tints. Its convex cap has a shallow dome that is slightly distorted. The cap peels off quite easily and is shiny to see and smooth to touch. The gills are crowded and attached to the stem that can be 5-8 centimeters long. The stem can be either yellow or white-colored.

The gills are light grey colored when young and change to take on a brownish hue when mature. The spores are almost globe-like and white in color.

Lyophyllum decastes/fried chicken mushroom/ chicken of the gravel

(7) Gypsy Mushroom

Gypsy mushrooms or cortinarius caperatus are pretty delicious and are found during the fall, along with coniferous trees and hardwoods.

These mushrooms are a pleasant sight with a toasted brown cap that can be 5-13 centimeters wide. When young, the caps are convex and slowly take on a bell-like shape as they mature. A fully matured mushroom of this variety has an almost flat cap with wrinkles.

These mushrooms start with a pale-yellow tinge and take on a yellowish-brown hue when young. These mushrooms have short and numerous gills that are attached to the stem. The gills are also pale but become darker and are closer to cinnamon brown color as they mature.

The stem can be 5-15 centimeters tall with fine longitudinal fibers and the upper portion. The thick white ring located on the upper part of the stem is one of its identifying features. The ellipsoidal spores of this mushroom have a rusty brown color.

cortinarius caperatus

Illustration by Albin Schmalfuß, 1897B
Public Domain, https://commons.wikimedia.org/w/index.php?curid=1229501

(8) Common Laccaria

Common laccaria or laccaria laccata are edible mushrooms commonly found across the globe in forests, bogs, and leaf litter on the forest floor. They prefer coniferous and broadleaf trees such as oaks, pines, beeches, and birches. The fruiting season for this mushroom is spring and fall in northern America. When young, these mushrooms have a convex cap that flattens out as they mature. A fully mature cap of this mushroom can be 2-6 centimeters wide.

The cap takes on a reddish-brown or a dark tan color during the rainy season and becomes lighter as the weather dries out.

The cap takes on a funnel-like shape with widely spaced large gills as the mushroom matures. The stem can be 2-10 centimeters long. This mushroom is also known as a deceiver because its appearance changes depending on climatic conditions.

The globular spores are white-colored. These mushrooms taste pretty similar to the regular button mushrooms found in the supermarket and are a perfect addition to stews, soups, and stir-fries.

Common laccaria

Image by Johnnys_pic from Pixabay

(9) Fairy Ring Mushroom

Fairy ring mushrooms or Marasmius oreades are quite scrumptious and commonly found in grasslands during spring and fall. The cap is 2-5 centimeters wide with tiny grooves along its margins. The cap can be light tan, orange, or cream-colored. When young, the gills are white-colored and turn cream as it matures. The gills are easily identifiable because they are free and distant from one another.

 At times, this mushroom is believed to resemble a fried egg with a yolk at its center and margins that slightly curl upward in most cases.

The stem is a pale shade of white and can be 4-8 centimeters long. It has white ellipsoidal spores. These mushrooms are also known as resurrection mushrooms because even if they look completely shriveled and dried up during peak summers, they regain their color once hydrated after rains.

Marasmius oreades

(10) Inky Cap

Inky cap or coprinopsis atramentaria are edible mushrooms but become poisonous when consumed with alcohol.

Ideally, refrain from eating these mushrooms three days before or after drinking alcohol.

These inky cap mushrooms are quite common and can be found in areas where the soil is regularly disturbed, such as pastures, abandoned lots, and lawns. They usually crop up from spring to fall.

These mushrooms are a treat to look at. Their grey-brown cap with inky black gills is the distinguishing feature. When young, the cap is egg-shaped and covered with small flat scales in the center. As it matures, the cap takes on a bell shape and turns grayish-brown before taking on a unique black hue. The cap is 3-7 centimeters wide with a stem that is 5-12 centimeters long.

The gills also change their colors, turning from a pristine white to a slightly brown and black. The mushroom looks like a partially closed umbrella with brownish grey, black, or dark grey hues. It has almond-shaped spores that are black too. The texture of this mushroom is dry and slightly silky and smooth to touch.

coprinopsis atramentaria

(11) Brown Double-Ringed Shaggy Parasol

Brown double-ringed shaggy parasol or chlorophyllum olivieri are delicious mushrooms but are not ideal for anyone with gastric troubles. When it is not properly cooked, it might trigger allergic reactions in some. It can be commonly found in all forest regions and backyards across the Pacific Northwest, and they appear during spring and fall.

The caps can be 7-14 centimeters wide and have a spherical shape when young. As the mushroom matures, the cap starts flattening and looks more and more like an open umbrella. The center of its cap is smooth and brown with visible scales that spread away from the center. The caps take on light brownish color as they mature. This mushroom has a double ring along its hollow stem that can be 9-14 centimeters long with a bulbous base.

The spores of this mushroom can be yellow or white. Whenever these mushrooms are cut or bruised, the color of their flesh changes immediately. Their white flesh turns bright orange or takes on a pinkish hue as soon as it is cut.

shaggy parasol or chlorophyllum olivieri

(12) White Matsutake

White matsutake or Tricholoma Magnivelare has a unique taste and is highly coveted in the culinary world. These delicious mushrooms have a sweet cinnamon-like taste with hints of cypress and a mild spicy kick. Whether these mushrooms are simply grilled or infused into soups and broths, they are versatile and absolutely tasty.

These mushrooms are usually found in coniferous forests during the month of fall across the Pacific Northwest. The cap of these mushrooms is 5-20 centimeters wide and is pristine white when they emerge for the first time. Eventually, it starts flattening out and developing tan lines and reddish-brown scales. It also has a flatter appearance as it matures. The gills are placed close together and firmly attached to the stipe.

In young mushrooms, the gills are cream-colored and take on a tan hue as they grow. The stipe can be 4-15 centimeters tall with a white veil that breaks irregularly. The globular spores are white-colored. Because these mushrooms are quite coveted for noncommercial or incidental use, only up to 6 of them can be foraged, according to Siuslaw National Forest.

White matsutake

(13) Shaggy Mane

Shaggy mane or Coprinus comatus are commonly found across open woodlands, meadows, and the roadside during late fall and summer. These mushrooms appear directly out of the ground and are quite scrumptious to eat. Ensure that these mushrooms are cooked and consumed quickly after foraging because their caps and gills are autodigestive. They are also known as shaggy inky caps and closely resemble the inky cap mushrooms. However, they are more common than regular inky caps. They start with an egg-shaped cap when young that is pure white.

It slowly takes on a brownish hue and breaks into large scales as they mature. The cap has scales cropping out from its surface when the weather is hot, and they flatten out when it rains. The cap by itself is 4-8 centimeters wide and can be up to 20 centimeters tall when fully mature. The gills are crowded and go from white to pink and ultimately black as they mature.

The stem can be anywhere between 30- 40 centimeters tall when fully mature. The stem has a double ring pattern on it, and its base is hollow and fibrous. The ellipsoidal spores are black too. The distinguishing feature between regular inky caps that can be dangerous and the shaggy inky cap is the shaggy section present in the center of the cap. Also, shaggy manes fly solo while inky caps appear in clusters.

Shaggy mane or Coprinus comatus

(14) White Double-Ringed Shaggy Parasol

White double-ringed shaggy parasols or chlorophyllum rhacodes are incredibly delicious mushrooms but are not ideal for anyone with gastric troubles.

They are commonly found in coniferous forests, shrubberies, and woods during summer and fall. They can appear in clusters or sprout individually. The cap of these mushrooms is initially 5-20 centimeters wide and has an oval shape.

It is also smooth and pink colored or slightly brown. As it matures, the cap opens up and slowly flattens and whitens. It develops shaggy brown scales too. The gills are crowded but free from the stem and change from white to tan as the mushroom matures. The stem has a smooth surface with a double annulus that freely moves up and down its length.

Compared to the top of the stem, its base is bulbous and can be 10-20 centimeters tall and up to 2.5 centimeters wide. It has ellipsoidal spores that are white-colored.

chlorophyllum rhacodes

(15) Deer Mushroom

Deer mushroom or pluteus cervinus is usually considered to be an edible mushroom, but there have been reports of some falling ill after eating them. It's also used as a condiment once dehydrated and grated for culinary purposes. These mushrooms favor hardwoods and can also be found on wood chips in urban landscapes. They flourish during spring and fall. The cap of these mushrooms is 4-10 centimeters wide. Its usual color ranges from sepia to a light brown reminiscent of deers with darker radial streaks running across it.

The mushroom cap is convex to begin with and eventually flattens out. It has white, crowded gills that mature as they take on a pink hue. The stem is 5-13 centimeters tall and has dark longitudinal fibers running toward the base of its white stem. The odor of these mushrooms is quite similar to that of radishes, and it has white flesh that does not bruise easily. The ellipsoidal spores are pale pink colored.

pluteus cervinus

Image by arttupulkkinenn from Pixabay

(16) Pacific Golden Chanterelle

Pacific golden chanterelle or Cantharellus formosus is an incredibly delicious variety of mushrooms native to the Pacific Northwest. It is also known as the state mushroom of Oregon. It usually grows among Douglas fir, spruce, and hemlock. They can either be found in small clusters or grow solitarily. The ideal season for foraging these mushrooms is early fall until mid-winter. Chanterelles are amongst the prettiest mushrooms you will come across. These mushrooms have an orange-yellow funnel-shaped cap. The cap has blunt ridges branching into wavy margins.

The fruiting body of this mushroom can be 10-14 centimeters wide, and its color varies according to the season. For instance, these mushrooms are light yellow-brown or yellowish-orange when the weather is dry. However, they take on a soft orange-yellow hue as soon as it rains. The undersurface of the cap has false gills running down the stem. The stem can be 4-6 centimeters tall and colored similarly to the cap. The ellipsoid spores can be white or pale-yellow colored. These chanterelles have a sweet smell.

The irregular and veiny gills and long and narrow stems are its defining features apart from its fruiting body.

Pacific golden chanterelle
Photo by Timothy Dykes on Unsplash

(17) The Prince Mushroom

The prince mushroom or Agaricus Augustus are incredibly delicious and are found along deciduous woodland zones and coniferous forest edges. The ideal time for foraging these mushrooms is early summer until fall. These mushrooms have an almost earthy smell and taste.

The right time to forage them is when their caps are still young. The cap of this mushroom can be 10-25 centimeters wide, and in certain instances, it can be up to 30 centimeters wide. It can have a 10-20-centimeter-long stem.

The cream-colored cap is covered with reddish-brown scales with pale pink gills attached to its stem. The pink gills turn dark purple as the mushroom matures. Its ellipsoidal spores are purple-brown too. It is said that these mushrooms derive their name from the month during which they grow — August.

If a specific recipe calls for Portobello mushrooms, you can use the prince mushrooms instead. Its earthy flavor profile will perfectly complement any meat-based dish.

Prince Mushroom or Agaricus Augustus

(18) Meadow Mushroom

Meadow mushrooms or Agaricus Campestris are extremely delicious and have a fleshy texture similar to regular button mushrooms. As their name suggests, these mushrooms are commonly found in meadows, fields, and lawns.

They are found between spring and winter. Usually, they are pretty abundant after rains. They either grow in clusters or solitarily. The creamy white cap of these mushrooms is shaped like a hemisphere and is 3-10 centimeters wide.

The cap is round, to begin with and starts flattening as the mushroom matures. The stem is 3-10 centimeters tall. It has radiating gills that look pink at first and take on a dark-brown hue as they grow.

The spores of these mushrooms are dark brown colored. A notable feature is they have a pleasant earthy aroma. Most of this mushroom's life cycle is spent in the soil as mycelium where it starts digesting and decomposing organic matter.

Meadow mushrooms or Agaricus Campestris **36**

(19) White Chanterelle

White Chanterelle or Cantharellus Subalbidus are delicious mushrooms that grow during fall and winter in the Pacific Northwest. You'll find them close to pine trees, Douglas firs, and hemlocks in this region.

Young white chanterelle mushrooms have a creamy white fruiting body that slowly turns yellow and orange as it matures. The cap is 5-10 centimeters wide, while the stem can be 2-5 centimeters tall. When compared to the top, the base of the stem is narrow.

When the stem bruises, it takes on an orange or yellow hue as the mushroom matures. False gills are present on the undersurface of the cap extending downward along the stem.

These false gills are often forked and highly corrugated. The ellipsoid spores are white-colored. Its meaty texture makes these mushrooms quite appealing.

White Chanterelle or Cantharellus Subalbidus

(20) Horn Of Plenty

Horn of plenty or craterellus cornucopioides is considered one of the tastiest chanterelles found in Europe and not just the Pacific Northwest. They commonly grow solitarily or in scattered groups. You can find these along with conifers and deciduous trees.

There is no apparent mark separating this mushroom's cap from its base. Usually, the fruiting body can be 10-15 centimeters tall. These mushrooms have a funnel-shaped fruiting body and resemble a trumpet. The diameter of the cap can be 4-8 centimeters wide. These mushrooms come in various colors ranging from dark grey and greyish-brown to black. Rarely, they are also yellow-colored.

The outer part of the cap is covered with fine wrinkles. The ellipsoid spores are white or cream-colored. Their unique appearance, coupled with their colors, makes it relatively easy to identify these mushrooms.

Horn of Plenty or Craterellus Cornucopioides

(21) Winter Chanterelle

Winter Chanterelles or Craterellus Tubaeformis are tasty mushrooms that grow solitarily or in groups with conifers. They usually grow during the winter months. The fruiting body of these chanterelles is 2-7 centimeters wide with a brownish-yellow cap.

The cap has a depressed center giving them a funnel-like appearance. The cap's margins are wavy and irregular. When fresh, these mushrooms are sticky to touch. As with other chanterelles, even they have cross-veined and forked gills extending downward from the top of the stem.

When young, the stem has a yellowish-orange hue and takes on a brownish tinge as it matures. The stem is hollow and can be 3-9 centimeters long. The elliptical spores are white or pale yellow colored. The deep depression in the mushroom cap makes them look like exotic tropical flowers.

They are rich in a variety of B-complex vitamins known for reducing inflammation, promoting bone health, and reducing the risk of diabetes. They are also rich in potassium, phosphorus, iron, and healthy dietary fiber.

Winter Chanterelles or Craterellus Tubaeformis

(22) Pig's Ear Gomphus

Pig's ear gomphus or gomphus clavatus is another variety of extremely delicious chanterelles. They either grow solitarily or in clusters during the fall in coniferous forests. The lobed cap can be up to 10 centimeters wide with an irregular outline. These mushrooms are convex when young and eventually develop light or a deep depression in their center. They will feel dry to touch and have tiny scales peppered on their surface. When fresh, these mushrooms are light brown colored with a hint of lilac. This color fades and takes on a cream-colored hue later. The flesh of this mushroom can be white or yellowish.

The cross-veined undersurface/bottom of the cap is extremely wrinkly and is purple or dark lilac-colored. It has ellipsoid and yellow-colored spores. The stem can be 2-4 centimeters long and is slightly lilac toward the top and white close to the base. Usually, you will find two or more irregularly shaped fruits growing from a single stem. Ensure that you thoroughly clean these mushrooms because bugs and insects love them as much as humans.

By Albin Schmalfuß - Führer für Pilzfreunde : die am häufigsten vorkommenden essbaren, verdächtigen und giftigen Pilze / von Edmund Michael ; mit 68 Pilzgruppen, nach der Natur von A. Schmalfuss [1] https://dx.doi.org/10.5962/bhl.title.3898, Public Domain, https://commons.wikimedia.org/w/index.php?curid=1290992

gomphus clavatus

(23) Blue Chanterelle

Blue chanterelle or polyozellus multiplex are extremely scrumptious edible mushrooms in old coniferous forests along the Pacific Northwest. The ideal time to forage these mushrooms is during summer and fall.

If you are heading out during these months, ensure that you look under conifers for these delicious mushrooms. This mushroom's purplish-gray or dark blue cap can be up to 10 centimeters wide. It has a lobed and wrinkly margin with scalloped edges. The outer part of the cap is smooth to touch, while its undersurface is extremely wrinkly.

The stem is 3-5 centimeters long and is the same color as the cap. These mushrooms have irregularly shaped spores that are white-colored. Their wonderful flavor and aroma make them a brilliant addition to sauces.

Blue chanterelle or polyozellus multiplex

(24) Woolly Chanterelle

Woolly chanterelle or turbinellus floccosus are edible but not for those with gastrointestinal troubles. These are commonly found in coniferous forests in the Pacific Northwest during fall and late summer.

Looking at this mushroom from the side, it has a vase-like structure. The orange hue of the cap makes it look like a tropical flower. The fleshy cap has a depression in its center that can be shallow or deep. The cap is 4-11 centimeters wide and can be 6-14 centimeters tall. The top part of this mushroom has soft scales with some yellow spots on it.

It has a fine and wavy margin, while its underside has long veins that run from the top of the cap to the base of the stem. The stem is 4-10 centimeters tall and is firmly attached to the cap. It is the same color as the underside of the cap. The flesh of this mushroom is surprisingly white. The ellipsoid spores are orange-yellow or yellowish.

Woolly chanterelle or turbinellus floccosus

(25) Rainbow Chanterelle

Rainbow chanterelle or Cantharellus roseocanus are tasty mushrooms that grow in conifer forests during summer and fall in the Pacific Northwest.

The yellowish-orange colored cap is 2.5-10 centimeters wide. When these mushrooms are young, their cap is convex shaped with the edges curving inward. As the mushroom matures, the cap also flattens and develops a mild depression in the center.

The color of the mushroom takes on an off-white hue when exposed to the sun or when growing in a sunny spot. It becomes sticky when exposed to rainfall. The stipe is 2-5 centimeters long and is the same color as the cap. However, the flesh does not bruise when cut but becomes slightly brown. The flesh of these brightly colored mushrooms is white on the inside.

The ellipsoid pores are pale orange or yellow. These mushrooms have an apricot-like sweet fragrance. However, even though they smell sweet, they have a peppery taste.

Rainbow chanterelle or Cantharellus roseocanus

(26) Cascade Chanterelle

Cascade chanterelle or Cantharellus cascadensis are commonly found in conifer forests and prefer hemlocks and Douglas firs.

You can usually forage for them in fall and early winter. These tasty wild mushrooms are a visual delight too. Its large cap is the color of an egg yolk. The fruiting body of this mushroom looks flat with wavy margins. The cap can be 4-12 centimeters wide. The convex shape of young cascade chanterelles has margins that roll inward. As the mushroom ages, the cap's edge starts rolling outward. The stem can be 2-10 centimeters along.

The base of the stem is fibrous and bulbous. It has shallow gills too. You will notice ridge-like veins from the edge of the cap to the top of the stipe. The thick and distant veins fork outward. These mushrooms have smooth white-colored spores.

(27) Scaly Chanterelle

Scaly chanterelle or turbinellus kauffmanii are commonly found in coniferous forests and are native to the Pacific Northwest region, including Northern California. They are quite common in the eastern states with hot and rainy summers. You will also find them during late autumn and early winter in the western regions of the Pacific Northwest. The edibility of this mushroom is not yet clear. That said, it contains norcaperatic acid that causes problems with the functioning of the central nervous system and skeletal muscles.

This mushroom has a unique vase-like shape with a fruiting body 10-20 centimeters wide. In some varieties, it can be up to 35 centimeters wide too.

The cap is usually brown with a tinge of olive in it. The surface is split into large scales. When young, the spore-bearing surface of this mushroom is yellow and takes on a pinkish hue when mature. The stem is 8-15 centimeters tall, but in some varieties, it can also be up to 40-centimeters tall. This mushroom has off-white spores. An interesting feature of these mushrooms is their pungent smell.

Cascade chanterelle or Cantharellus cascadensis

Scaly chanterelle or turbinellus kauffmanii

Inedible or Poisonous Mushrooms

As a forager, you should not only learn about the mushrooms you can eat. You must also learn about the ones you should stay away from. In this section, look at the most common species of inedible and poisonous mushrooms found in the Pacific Northwest.

(1) False Chanterelles

False chanterelle or hygrophoropsis aurantiaca is an inedible mushroom and is commonly found on rotting conifers during summer and fall in the Pacific Northwest.

These mushrooms have yellow, orange-brown, or orange-colored caps that can be 0.5-9 centimeters wide. The cap can be flat, convex, or depressed, with gills growing down its stem. The gills are quite narrow and placed close together, and the stem can be 2.5-10 centimeters tall. The cap margins are irregular and roll inward. These mushrooms have ellipsoidal spores that are cream or white-colored. They are commonly confused with chanterelles that are quite delicious. The difference between these is in the shape and color of their caps.

False chanterelle or hygrophoropsis aurantiaca

(2) Rosy Gomphidius

Rosy gomphidius mushrooms or gomphidius subroseus are inedible mushroom species. Please stay away from it because its flesh has significant traces of heavy metals picked up from its surroundings.

These mushrooms are commonly found under conifers and have a special preference for Douglas fir. These mushrooms can be seen from early fall until mid-winter. These mushrooms' bright pink or reddish-pink cap is 3-6 centimeters wide. It is slimy and sticky to touch. When young, these mushrooms have a convex-shaped cap that slowly flattens out and forms a little depression in the center.

These are extremely small mushrooms, and their stem is 3-9 centimeters tall and white-colored with a yellow base. Their gills run down on either side of the stipe and start with a pale color but eventually turn grey. These mushrooms have narrow ellipsoidal spores that are black or grayish-purple.

Gomphidius roseus/ rosy spike-cap or pink gomphidius

(3) Slimy Gomphidius

Slimy gomphidius or gomphidius glutinosus is an edible mushroom with a high concentration of heavy metals in its flesh. As with rosy gomphidius, even the slimy gomphidius prefers conifer forests and blooms during the fall.

They can either grow in clumps or alone. The cap of these mushrooms can be 3-12 centimeters wide and looks like the top of a child's toy. The dark grey or purple cap is convex when young and flattens out as it matures. It might also develop some black markings at this stage.

As the name suggests, the surface of this mushroom is rather sticky to touch. Its stem can be 3-10cm tall and has distant gills that are far apart from each other. The gills are white to begin with and eventually turn black as the mushroom matures. Its spindle-shaped spores are blackish-brown colored.

Gomphidius glutinosus or slimy spike-cap

(4) Man On Horseback

Man on horseback or tricholoma equestre are extremely poisonous, and you should stay away from them at all costs. These mushrooms prefer coniferous forests and are found during late summer and fall.

In some parts of the Pacific Northwest, they can be found until winter sets in. These mushrooms have a broadly convex cap that can be 3-15 centimeters wide and is usually yellow-colored with a tinge of brown mixed in, especially in the middle. The cap's edges roll inward when young and slowly flatten out as it matures.

The young mushrooms have a sticky cap that slowly dries out with age. The gills have notched margins and are medium spaced. The gills are a pale yellow color. The stem is yellowish-green itself and is 3-10 centimeters long. The flesh of this mushroom can be clear yellow or white, depending on its maturity. These poisonous mushrooms have elliptical white-colored spores.

Man on horseback or Tricholoma Equestre

(5) Western Flat-Topped Agaricus

Western flat-topped Agaricus or Agaricus Moelleri are poisonous mushrooms commonly found in woodlands. They usually grow in late summer and fall. They can grow singularly or in small clusters.

Their caps are off-white-colored and 3-1- centimeters wide in diameter. The cap has grey-brown scales in the center and is covered with greyish or dark brown fibers. Initially, the cap is globose or rounded and slowly takes on a convex shape as the mushroom matures.

The stem is 6-10 centimeters tall. The upper portion of the stem has a pendulous ring that stays present throughout the mushroom's lifecycle. These mushrooms have free gills that are set close together. Initially, the gills are pinkish colored and take on a brown-black appearance later.

It is said that these mushrooms have an intense smell, especially when cut or crushed. As soon as the stem is cut, its color changes from white to yellow. The ellipsoidal spores are brown-colored. These mushrooms are named after a German mycologist and a forest botanist named Alfred Moller.

Agaricus Moelleri

(6) Death Cap

Death cap or amanita phalloides are extremely poisonous mushrooms and should be avoided at all costs. Please be careful because there is no known antidote for this mushroom's poison. The most common poisoning symptoms include nausea, severe stomach cramps, palpitations, excess sweating, and diarrhea. The symptoms can be felt within 6-24 hours after eating a death cap mushroom. Even if the symptoms subside, the toxic compounds are still present within the system and can wreak havoc within 3-5 days of consumption resulting in various organ failures followed by death.

These mushrooms are commonly found under hardwood trees such as pine, birch, spruce, and oak. They thrive in forests, especially after rains. They can also be found in open and grassy patches in urban areas. This mushroom is native to Europe but was introduced to North America along with the trees it uses as a host. They are commonly found in all regions of the Pacific Northwest. This is one mushroom you should be extremely careful with.

The mushroom has a distinct greenish cap with a skirt-like ring in the upper portion of the stem. It has white gills. The stem has a bulbous base. When it comes to identifying this mushroom, you need to inspect all parts of it, including the base of its stem.

The cap of this mushroom can be 3-8 centimeters wide. It starts with a rounded shape, slowly flattens out, and takes on a convex shape as it matures. The color of the cap can be green, brown, or yellow. .

The center is usually darker than its margins. The cap might initially look smooth but has fine white notches on it. These patches are the remnants of the veil

When you look closely at this mushroom, you'll notice it has a satiny shine that makes it slippery after rains. The gills are free from the stem or are narrowly attached to it. The stem can be 5-13 centimeters tall and is always wider at the base and narrow at the top. The gills are initially covered in a veil but result in the creation of a skirt-like structure toward the upper part of the stem when mature.

These mushrooms have elliptical spores that are white and smooth. When the spores are mixed with Melzer's iodine reagent, they turn blue. Apart from the spore print, you must look for its characteristic white gills that do not change color, a large skirt, a cap with a green or yellow tinge, and a cup-like volva at the base. Once you notice all these four features in a mushroom, stay away from it.

Death cap or amanita phalloides

(7) Fly Amanita

Fly amanita or amanita muscaria is a poisonous mushroom and a known hallucinogen. These mushrooms are commonly found in coniferous forests, especially birch and pine trees.

They are abundant during the fall but can be found late in summer. These mushrooms look like something right out of a fairytale. However, even though they are quite pretty to look at, these mushrooms should be avoided because they are poisonous. They have a red or orange cap that can be 10-20 centimeters wide. The cap has small white protrusions on it.

Initially, the cap is globulus, to begin with, and starts flattening out as the mushroom matures. The stem can be 12-20 centimeters tall with a bulbous base. The veil covers the gills as the mushroom develops.

The remnants of this veil can be found between the gills and toward the base of the stem. It has white gills that are free of the stem. The oval spores of this mushroom are white-colored. The toxins present in this mushroom directly affect the nervous system and can result in coma and death in extreme cases. The most common symptoms of poisoning caused by these mushrooms include dizziness, confusion, nausea, vomiting, changes in visual and auditory perception, and a lack of awareness of time. The symptoms can last between 8-24 hours after consumption.

Fly amanita or amanita muscaria

4. Preserving and Storing Mushrooms

Mushrooms are a part of different culinary traditions across the globe. The texture and taste of most mushrooms can quickly elevate any dish you are cooking. Their earthy aroma and taste make them an ideal pairing for meat-based dishes. These nutritious ingredients could soon boost your meal's flavor and nutrient profile.

An important aspect of becoming a forager is not just learning to forage mushrooms. After all, what is the point of spending hours searching for mushrooms if you don't enjoy them? This is where the concept of cooking and preserving mushrooms steps into the picture.

Foraging Mushroom   Preserving Mushroom

Whether it is a soup, pasta, stew, or salad, fresh mushrooms can be added to various dishes. Most taste incredible when sautéed with a bit of butter and aromatics or grilled and fried.

Regardless of the recipe, you want to experiment with, ensure that you always cook the mushroom before eating. Mushrooms should never be consumed in their raw form.

Even though certain species can be eaten right away, it's always better to cook them. This is because mushrooms have rigid cellular walls that are indigestible when uncooked. Also, the nutrients present in mushrooms break free easily and offer better absorption of the vitamins and minerals present when exposed to heat.

Apart from this, any natural toxins, allergens, or irritants present in the mushrooms are also eliminated when cooked.

If you are trying a specific mushroom for the first time, it's better that you do not drink alcohol. This is especially true for certain mushroom varieties discussed in this book. Alcohol may trigger a stronger allergic reaction to mushrooms, especially those of the Coprinus genus (commonly known as shaggy mane mushrooms).

Ideally, avoid consuming mushrooms three days before or after drinking alcohol. It might trigger unpleasant symptoms such as vomiting, nausea, sweating, diarrheal, and palpitations.

Ensure that you thoroughly clean the mushrooms before you start cooking with them.

This is crucial for any foods that have been foraged in the wild. The smooth skin-like surface of mushrooms is waterproof; therefore, most species can be washed without a problem. However, if the specific variety of mushrooms you are handling is absorbent, cleaning it for prolonged periods is not a good idea because it tends to lose flavor and become soggy when placed in water. Instead, a soft-bristled brush helps eliminate the dirt and debris to preserve its crispness. After this, a soft wet cloth can clean the dirty surface.

Mushroom cleaning by water

If you have foraged more mushrooms than you can consume them right away or want to store some, preserving them is crucial. The ideal way to keep mushrooms is by dehydrating or freezing them.

Certain mushrooms are suited for canning and pickling as well. Ideally, dehydrating the mushrooms ensures their aroma and flavors stay intact. They can also be rehydrated when added to soups and pasta. Dried mushrooms can also be turned into powders that can be used as a seasoning. You don't need any special air-drying equipment. Instead, clean the mushrooms, and hang them to dry in a room or an area with sufficient airflow. If you have a dehydrator, it makes the entire process quicker.

Canned Mushroom

Pickled Mushroom

Mushroom Powder

Two options are available for storing mushrooms, and they are freezing and drying.

Both are commonly used and work well for most species of mushrooms. Once the mushrooms are dried, place them in an airtight jar or a plastic bag to prolong their shelf life. If the mushrooms are sliced too thinly or crushed finely, vacuum sealing might not work. Once you have placed the mushrooms in airtight containers, ensure they are vacuum-sealed.

Dried mushrooms can be stored between 6-12 months when appropriately sealed.

The other option that can be used for preserving mushrooms is freezing. This does not alter their fiber or calorie content. However, the texture is slightly altered due to their high water content affected by freezing.

Some mushrooms can become mushy or softer when frozen and thawed. So, if you want to use frozen mushrooms, they are well suited for soups, stews, and curries instead of any recipe that calls for sautéing. Freezing mushrooms is quite convenient. You simply need to place the cleaned mushrooms in an airtight bag such as a ziplock bag and place them in a freezer. These can last anywhere between 6-12 months when stored properly.

5. Let's Cook - Wild Mushroom Recipes

(1) Mushroom Chutney/Salad

Serves: 8 – 10

Ingredients:

- 4 cups split-gill mushrooms, cleaned, rinsed well

- 2 – 10 green chilies, depending on how hot to prefer

- ½ teaspoon salt or to taste

- 2 bunches hooker chives or garlic chives, rinsed, chopped into 1-inch pieces

- 4 large tomatoes, cored

- Water as required

Directions:

1.   Place mushrooms in a pan. Add a cup of water and a little salt and place the pan over medium heat. Cook until dry. Turn off the heat and transfer into a bowl.

2.   Pierce the green chilies with a fork at different places. Place green chilies and tomatoes on a grill pan and grill until the tomatoes are slightly charred and the chilies have blisters on them. It would taste wonderful if you could roast them on a charcoal grill.

3. Remove the chilies from the pan when it has blisters and continue cooking the tomatoes until charred. Finally, peel the tomatoes and chop them into chunks.

4.   Place chilies and tomatoes in a blender and blend until coarsely ground.

5.   Pour the blended mixture into the bowl of mushrooms. Mix well and serve.

6.   You can serve this with rice or spread it as a filling for sandwiches or wraps.

Mushroom Salad

Photo by Ella Olsson: https://www.pexels.com/photo/vegetable-salad-3026808/

(2) Mushroom Tea of Split Gill

Serves: 2

Ingredients:

- 14 split-gill mushrooms, fresh or dried
- 4 cups of water
- 2 teaspoons honey (optional)

Directions:

1. Pour water into a saucepan and heat it over high heat. When water starts boiling, add the mushrooms and lower the heat. Cook for about 30 – 40 minutes.

2. Strain and serve in cups adding honey if desired. You may not like the taste of the tea, so I recommend you add honey or some fruit juice to taste.

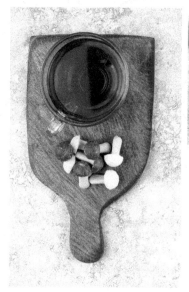

Mushroom Tea

(3) Wild Mushrooms with Breadcrumbs, Garlic, and Chili

Serves: 5 – 6

Ingredients:

- 1 pound fresh wild mushrooms like split-gill or slippery jacks
- 6 tablespoons unsalted butter
- ½ cup panko breadcrumbs
- 4 cloves garlic, crushed along with skin
- Salt to taste
- 4 tablespoons cooking oil or lard
- Pepper to taste
- 2 teaspoons crushed red pepper
- 2 teaspoons fresh chopped thyme

Directions:

1. Pour oil into a pan and let it heat over medium heat. When oil is hot, add garlic and cook until light brown.

2. Stir in butter and mushrooms and cook until mushrooms are light brown.

3. Add salt and pepper to taste. Lower the heat and stir in the breadcrumbs and thyme. Mix well.

4. Cook until the breadcrumbs turn golden brown. Stir often. Turn off the heat.

5. Add crushed red pepper and stir.

6. Serve right away. This can be served as a snack or side dish, or appetizer.

Wild Mushrooms with Breadcrumbs

(4) Simple Sautéed Chanterelle Mushrooms

Serves: 2

Ingredients:

- ½ tablespoon olive oil
- 1 clove of garlic, minced
- ½ tablespoon butter
- Pepper to taste
- ½ large shallot, finely chopped
- ½ pound chanterelle mushrooms
- 1/8 teaspoon salt or to taste

Sautéed Chanterelle Mushrooms

Directions:

1. Pour oil into a pan and place it over medium-high heat. When oil is hot, add shallots and cook until they turn soft.

2. Lower the heat and cook until light brown. Stir in garlic and cook for a couple of minutes. Transfer the onion mixture onto a plate.

3. Add more oil if required. Add mushrooms and a bit of salt and stir. Spread the mushrooms all over the pan and let it cook undisturbed for a couple of minutes.

4. Stir and spread it once again. Cook for another 2 – 3 minutes.

5. Add butter and stir. Cook for a couple of minutes.

6. Mix in the shallots. Add some salt and pepper to taste.

7. Serve.

(5) Gorgonzola and Wild Mushroom Risotto

Serves: 2

Ingredients:

- 1 ounce dried chanterelle mushrooms
- Hot water to soak the mushrooms
- ½ teaspoon truffle oil (optional)
- 1 shallot, minced
- 1 ½ ounce sliced fresh edible wild mushrooms of your choice
- ¼ cup dry white wine
- 1 tablespoon heavy cream
- Pepper to taste
- 1 teaspoon butter
- ½ onion, chopped
- 2 small cloves of garlic, minced
- ½ package (from a 12 ounces package) Arborio rice
- 2 cups hot chicken stock
- 1 tablespoon crumbled Gorgonzola cheese or to taste

Directions:

1. Place chanterelle mushrooms in a bowl of hot water. Let it rehydrate for 30 minutes.

2. Drain the mushrooms and chop them into pieces.

3. Place a saucepan over medium-high heat. Add butter and truffle oil. When butter melts, add shallot, garlic, and onion and cook for a few minutes until soft.

4. Stir in the fresh mushrooms and cook until some moisture is released from the mushrooms.

5. Add chanterelle mushrooms and cook for 2 minutes.

6. Stir in the rice. Keep stirring for a few minutes.

7. Pour white wine and stir. Cook until almost dry.

8. Lower the heat and pour about a cup of the stock into the saucepan. Cook until nearly dry.

9. Repeat this process until all the stock is added. If the rice is not cooked when all the broth has been added, add a sprinkle of water and cook until al dente.

10. Turn off the heat. Add cream, salt, pepper, and cheese and mix well.

11. Serve hot.

Mushroom Risotto

(6) Mushroom Sauce

Serves: 8

Ingredients:

- 4 cups fresh sliced chanterelle mushrooms
- 1 cup chopped mushrooms of your choice
- ½ cup + 2 tablespoons butter
- 1/8 cup minced shallots
- 1 teaspoon dried thyme
- ½ cup red wine
- 2 tablespoons arrowroot powder
- Freshly ground black pepper to taste
- 2 bay leaves
- 4 cups beef broth or any other broth of your choice
- Salt to taste

Directions

1. Place a large pan over medium heat. Add ½ cup butter. When butter melts, add chanterelle mushrooms and cook until tender.

2. Transfer the mushrooms into a bowl.

3. Wipe the pan and add 2 tablespoons of butter into the pan. When butter melts, add shallots and cook until soft. Stir in chopped mushrooms and cook until tender.

4. Stir in bay leaves, thyme, and red wine and simmer until the wine is half its original quantity

5.   Whisk together arrowroot powder with ½ cup broth.

6.   Pour the remaining broth into the pan and let it come to a boil. When the mixture starts boiling, pour the arrowroot mixture into the pan and keep stirring until the sauce thickens.

7.   Stir in the chanterelle mushroom and heat thoroughly. Add salt and pepper to taste.

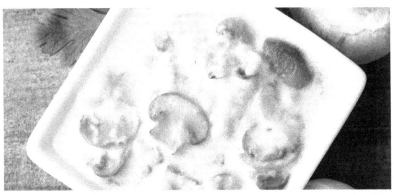

Mushroom Sauce

(7) Creamy Chanterelle Mushroom Soup

Serves: 8

Ingredients:

- 16 ounces chanterelle mushrooms, rinsed well
- 4 cups diced shallots
- 2 tablespoons olive oil
- 1 cup half and half
- ½ cup butter
- Salt to taste
- Pepper to taste
- 8 cups chicken stock

Directions:

1. Dry the mushrooms by patting them with paper towels or a kitchen towel. Cut them into smaller pieces.

2. Place a soup pot over medium heat. Add butter. When butter melts, add shallots and cook until they turn soft.

3. Add mushrooms and ½ teaspoon salt and stir. Stir in oil and pepper. Cook until the mushrooms turn light brown.

4. Add stock and stir. When it starts boiling, lower the heat and cook for about 18 – 20 minutes.

5. Turn off the heat. Cool for some time. Blend the soup in a blender until smooth.

6.   Pour half and half into the blender and blend until smooth.

7.   Pour the soup back into the pot and heat for about 10 minutes.

8.   Ladle into soup bowls and serve.

9.   Note: This soup can be made with any kind of mushroom, whether wild or regular.

Chanterelle Mushroom Soup

(8) Fresh Porcini or Bolete Julienne

Serves: 8

Ingredients:

- 8 ounces young porcini or any other bolete mushrooms, cleaned, trimmed, cut into ¼-inch thick slices
- 4 – 8 tablespoons dry white wine
- 1/8 cup garlic greens
- 4 teaspoons all-purpose flour
- ½ cup grated parmesan cheese or Grana Padano cheese
- ½ teaspoon minced fresh thyme (optional)
- 4 tablespoons cooking oil
- ½ cup diced yellow onion
- 2 tablespoons unsalted butter
- ½ cup sour cream
- ½ cup grated gruyere
- 1/8 teaspoon freshly grated nutmeg

Directions:

1. Set the temperature of the oven to 375 degrees F.

2. Pour 2 tablespoons of oil into a large pan and place it over medium-high heat. When the oil is very hot, add mushrooms and cook until golden brown. Stir occasionally.

3. Remove the mushrooms from the pan and place them in a bowl. Add salt and pepper to taste.

4. Pour the remaining oil into the pan and let it heat over medium-low heat.

5.   When oil is hot, add onion and cook for a couple of minutes. Stir in the garlic and cook until the onions are soft.

6.   Add the mushrooms into the pan along with thyme and butter. When butter melts, add flour and nutmeg and stir. Cook for a minute or so until the flour is light brown.

7.   Pour wine into the pan. Scrape the bottom of the pan to remove any browned bits that may be stuck.

8.   Add sour cream, Gruyere cheese, and Parmesan cheese and mix well. Add some salt and pepper to taste if required. Simmer until the cheese melts, and you have a thick sauce. Turn off the heat.

9.   Spoon the mixture into a baking dish.

10. Place the baking dish in the oven and set the timer for 15 minutes or until brown at a few spots.

11. Remove the baking dish from the oven and let it cool for 5 minutes.

12. Serve.

Fresh Porcini or Bolete Julienne

6. Seasonal Calendar–
Pacific Northwest Mushrooms

(1) Seasonal Calendar - Wild Mushrooms of PNW

a) January

- Black Trumpet
- Chanterelle, Yellowfoot
- Hedgehog
- Truffle, Black
- Truffle, White

Black Trumpet

b) February

- Black Trumpet
- Hedgehog
- Truffle, Black

Morel

c) March

- Oyster
- Black Trumpet

d) April

- Morel
- Oyster

Oyster

e) May

- Boletus, King
- Coral Mushroom
- Morel
- Oyster
- Puffball
- Snowbank Mushroom

Boletus
Photo by Kostiantyn Li on Unsplash

f) June

- Boletus, King
- Coral Mushroom
- Morel
- Puffball
- Snowbank Mushroom

g) July

Western Giant Puffball

- Boletus, King
- Chanterelle
- Lobster
- Morel

h) August

- Cauliflower
- Chanterelle
- Chicken of the Woods
- Morel

Chanterelle

74

i) September

- Boletus, King
- Cauliflower
- Chanterelle
- Chicken of the Woods
- Honey Mushroom
- Matsutake

Chicken of Woods

j) October

- Angel Wings
- Boletus, King
- Fairy Ring
- Hawks Wing
- Man on Horseback
- Matsutake
- Saffron Milky Cap
- Snowbank Mushroom

Matsutake

k) November

- Black Trumpet
- Boletus, King
- Chanterelle
- Hedgehog
- Man on Horseback
- Matsutake
- Saffron Milky Cap
- Snowbank Mushroom
- The Prince

Angel Wings

1) December

- Black Trumpet
- Chanterelle, Yellowfoot
- Hedgehog
- Truffle, Black
- Truffle, White

Prince Mushrooms

How to harvest mushrooms correctly?

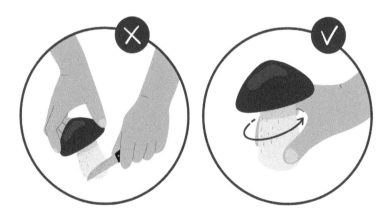

7. Conclusion

I want to thank you once again for choosing this book. I hope it proved to be an enjoyable and informative read.

If you reside in the Pacific Northwest, do not let go of any opportunities to head into the wild and forage mushrooms.

Mushroom foraging is a truly relaxing, engaging, exciting, and rewarding activity. With a little knowledge, patience, and a curious mind, you can quickly become a mushroom forager.

The Pacific Northwest's climatic and geographical conditions power the perfect environment for different species of mushrooms to grow and thrive.

Spend some time and learn more about the different species of edible mushrooms included in this book. You must have the required equipment, such as a magnifying glass and knife for identifying and harvesting the mushrooms.

Before you harvest, ensure that you're 100% certain of the mushroom, and it is not a poisonous lookalike. Some edible mushrooms are incredibly delicious, while others have medicinal properties. Learning about them is the only way to make the most of the helpful properties they offer.

This also ensures you are not harvesting inedible or poisonous mushrooms.

In this book, everything you need to know about foraging mushrooms in the wild is explained in detail. All you need to do is follow the five simple steps. With a little planning, preparation, and the right information, foraging becomes a rewarding activity. Do not forget to explore the different recipes given in this book using wild edible mushrooms. After all, it is not just about successfully foraging mushrooms but enjoying them is equally important.

Are you eager to get started? This book will act as your guide every step of the way and teach you everything you need about foraging edible mushrooms ethically and sustainably. The good news is it is never too late to learn something new.

So, what are you waiting for? Use the different information given in this book and start foraging edible mushrooms in the Pacific Northwest!

Thank you, and all the best!

Appendix - 1- Edible Mushrooms

EDIBLE MUSHROOMS SET

CEP

CHAMPIGNONS

AGARIC

OYSTER

SUILLUS

CORAL MILKY CAR

PORCINI

RUSSULA

LACTARIUS

ASPEN

CAESAR'S

MOREL

SAFFRON

SHIITAKE

CHANTERELLE

BLACK TRUFFLE

ENOKI

INDIGO
LACTARIUS

LION'S MANE
MUSHROOM

PUFFBALL

Appendix - 2- Spore Print

The Mushroom

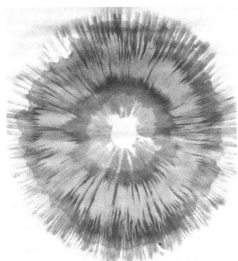

Spore Print

Appendix - 2- Identification Logbook

General Details

Date/Day _____

Weather ☐ ☐ ☐

Location/GPS _____

Temprature _____

By/Person _____

Growth Medium & Surrounding

Forest Type
☐ Coniferous ☐ Tropical ☐ Deciduous ☐ Others

Remarks _____

Growth Medium
☐ Soil ☐ Grass ☐ Dead Wood ☐ Tree

☐ Leaf ☐ Rocky Surface ☐ Mushroom ☐ Other

Remarks _____

Soil Type
☐ Clay ☐ Sandy ☐ Loam ☐ Others

Additional Information

Species/Type _____   Color _____

Specimen _____   Length _____

Cap Shape and Characterstics

☐ Conical ☐ Bell ☐ Funnel ☐ Umbonate ☐ Flat

☐ Hemispherical ☐ Umblicate ☐ Convex ☐ Oval ☐ Depression

☐ Conical Scale ☐ Knobbed ☐ Sunken ☐ Kidney ☐ Cone shaped revoluted

☐ sessile ☐ Helm ☐ Sub-globular ☐ Papillate ☐ Dimidiate

Additional Cap Information

Cap Diagram

Other details

Cap color ....

Cap shape ....

Cap texture ....

Cap diameter ....

Cap length ....

Hymenium ....

Cap surface

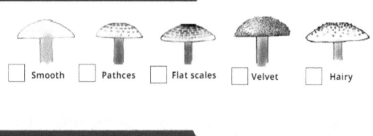

☐ Smooth ☐ Pathces ☐ Flat scales ☐ Velvet ☐ Hairy

Gills

☐ False Gills ☐ Teeth ☐ Pores ☐ Gills

☐ Close ☐ Spaced ☐ Intermediate ☐ Anastomosing

Additional Notes

Gill attachment to the stalk

Sketch

Example of free gill attachment

☐ **Free**
(Not attached)

☐ **Adnexed**
(Narrowly attached)

☐ **Sinuate**
(Notched before slightly running down)

☐ **Subdecurrent**
(Gills running slightly down the stem)

☐ **Emarginate**
Notched before attachment

☐ **Adnate**
Widely attached

☐ **Decurrent**
(Running down)

☐ **Seceding**
(Gills attached but breaking away)

Additional Notes

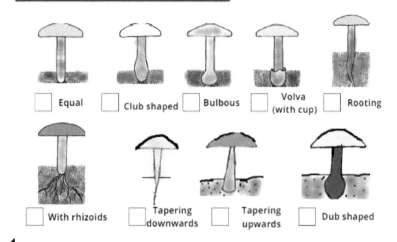

☐ Equal ☐ Club shaped ☐ Bulbous ☐ Volva (with cup) ☐ Rooting

☐ With rhizoids ☐ Tapering downwards ☐ Tapering upwards ☐ Dub shaped

Mushroom Ring Type

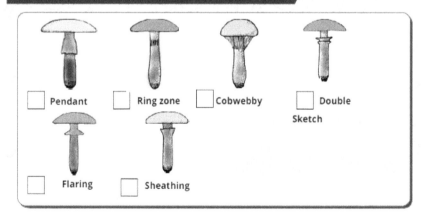

☐ Pendant ☐ Ring zone ☐ Cobwebby ☐ Double

Sketch

☐ Flaring ☐ Sheathing

ReFERENCES

Foraging: Ultimate Guide to Wild Food. (n.d.). Foraging for Wild Edibles. https://www.wildedible.com/foraging#:~:text=Use%20all%20of%20your%20senses.&text=Lots%20of%20wild%20edible%20 0

Hale, J. (2016, May 25). Can you identify the poisonous plants of the Pacific Northwest? Oregonlive. https://www.oregonlive.com/travel/2016/05/can_you_identif y_the_poisonous.html

Kloos, S. (2017, April 13). Wildcrafting Basics: Toxic Plants. The School of Forest Medicine. https://forestmedicine.net/ecological-intelligence-blog/2017/4/10/toxic-plants

Maxey, L. (2018, August 9). Foraging as a Route to Wellbeing. Network of Wellbeing. https://networkofwellbeing.org/2018/08/09/foraging-as-a-route-to-wellbeing/

Ovenden, S. (n.d.). Foraging: A beginner's guide. BBC Good Food. https://www.bbcgoodfood.com/howto/guide/foraging

Rezackova, L. (2020, July 2). 7 Amazing Benefits of Foraging for Wild Foods. Creativeedgetravel. https://www.creativeedgetravel.com/post/7-amazing-benefits-of-foraging-for-wild-foods

Selected Poisonous Plants of the Pacific Northwest | Animal Agriculture | Washington State University. (n.d.). Animal Agriculture. https://extension.wsu.edu/animalag/content/selected-poisonous-plants-of-the-pacific-northwest/

Wild Edible Plants of the Pacific Northwest. (n.d.). Www.northernbushcraft.com. https://www.northernbushcraft.com/plants/

Keough, B. (2020, July 13). Here's What You'll Need to Start Foraging Mushrooms. Wirecutter: Reviews for the Real World. https://www.nytimes.com/wirecutter/blog/how-to-hunt-mushrooms/

Rabins, I. (2020, April 23). Health Benefits of Mushroom Foraging. Book Wild Food Foraging Classes Online | ForageSF. https://www.foragesf.com/blog/2020/4/23/health-benefits-of-mushroom-foraging

Wayne, J. (2021, May 10). 5 Steps to Start Foraging. Center for Nutrition Studies. https://nutritionstudies.org/5-steps-to-start-foraging/

Wild Edible Mushrooms of British Columbia. (n.d.). Northernbushcraft.com. https://northernbushcraft.com/mushrooms/britishcolumbia.php

Wild Edible Mushrooms of the Pacific Northwest. (n.d.). Northernbushcraft.com. https://northernbushcraft.com/mushrooms/

We'd Love Your Feedback!

Please let us know how we're doing by leaving us a review.

Notes

Notes

Milton Keynes UK
Ingram Content Group UK Ltd.
UKHW020918201024
2274UKWH00033B/303